i-SPY

on the farm

SPY IT! SCORE IT!

Introduction

Almost everything you eat will have started out in some form on a farm, from wheat for the bread in your sandwiches to the apples in your fruit bowl. Visiting a farm is a good way to learn about where your food comes from and all the hard work involved in getting it on to your plate. You might encounter a farm on a countryside walk or maybe visit a farm park with your friends. These are fun places where you can learn about what farmers do, as well as taking part in fun activities. You might find some of the items in this book in a farm shop. Whatever kind of farm you visit, there's always so much to i-SPY along the way.

How to use your i-SPY book

Keep your eyes peeled for the i-SPYs in the book.

If you spy it, score it by ticking the circle or star.

Items with a star are difficult to spot so you'll have to search high and low to find them.

Once you score 1000 points, send away for your super i-SPY certificate. Follow the instructions on page 64 to find out how.

British landrace pig

These pigs have droopy ears and can live happily inside or out. They might look pink to you, but they are actually classed as white pigs.

15 POINTS

Gloucestershire old spot pig

Known for being excellent at foraging for food, these are white pigs with black spots – though the number of spots they have can vary.

25 POINTS

Tamworth pig

You might spot these pigs wallowing in mud on a hot day in order to cool down. They are covered with bristly, bronze-coloured hair.

20 POINTS

Saddleback pig

These pigs are easily recognised for their black bodies, which have a distinctive white stripe that extends down their front legs.

25 POINTS

Hebridean sheep

Small black sheep, originally from Scotland, Hebrideans are easily identified by their horns – while just one pair is usual, many of these sheep have two pairs.

TOP SPOT!

35 POINTS

Ryeland sheep

These sheep look a little like teddy bears with their round bodies and short wool. Their fleece has been prized for hundreds of years.

25 POINTS

Suffolk sheep

You can identify a Suffolk sheep by its black face and legs, and bell-shaped ears. They are farmed all over the UK and around the world.

15 POINTS

Welsh mountain sheep

These small white sheep are well suited to harsh mountain environments. Only the males (rams) have horns.

30 POINTS

Friesian cow

These are excellent dairy animals as they can produce large amounts of milk. They have distinctive black-and-white markings.

10 POINTS

Jersey cow

Prized for the quality of their milk, these golden-coloured cows are originally from Jersey, one of the Channel Islands, but can now be found around the world.

20 POINTS

Highland cow

This famous Scottish breed of cattle has a shaggy coat and often looks in need of a hair cut. It is mainly found in the Scottish Highlands and islands, though small herds can be found elsewhere in the UK, too.

30 POINTS

English longhorn cow

The long, curved horns of these beef cows were once used to make buttons, cups and cutlery – but fortunately this is no longer done.

35 POINTS

TOP SPOT!

Saanen goat

The largest dairy goat, the Saanen, is white in colour and is known for its excellent milk. Despite being one of the larger goat breeds, they are known for being friendly and calm.

15 POINTS

Pygmy goat

These goats are especially cute, with much stubbier legs and bodies than usual farm goats. They are more commonly kept as show animals, so you may see them in a farm's petting area.

TOP SPOT!

35 POINTS

Anglo-Nubian goat

The long, droopy ears of this goat make it very distinctive. Its milk is perfect for cheese and yoghurt.

25 POINTS

Tabby cat

Farm cats are often semi-wild and love their independence. You can identify a tabby cat by its markings – often black or dark brown stripes and swirls among lighter brown fur.

15 POINTS

Ginger cat

With a reputation for being vocal and friendly, these are among the most popular domestic cats. You might spot them snoozing in a patch of sunlight or in the shade of a barn.

20 POINTS

Border collie

These black-and-white dogs are commonly used by farmers to herd sheep and other livestock out in the field.

20 POINTS

Old English sheepdog

This incredibly fluffy breed was originally used to help drive sheep and cows to market. Their big coat requires a lot of grooming to keep it in good shape, but it helps keep them warm and waterproof.

TOP SPOT!

35 POINTS

German shepherd

Large brown-and-black dogs, German shepherds are excellent at herding sheep and guarding livestock.

25 POINTS

Huacaya alpaca

Originally from South America, these fluffy animals are usually kept for their soft fleece (wool), which can be made into jumpers, hats and rugs, among many other things.

35 POINTS

TOP SPOT!

Poitou donkey

There are thought to be only about 60 of these donkeys in the UK, but their small size, big ears and long, matted coat make them very distinctive. An adult male is known as a 'baudet'.

35 POINTS

Standard donkey

This is the most common kind of donkey you will see at a farm. Modern donkeys are descended from wild asses that lived in north and east Africa thousands of years ago.

10 POINTS

Shire horse

TOP SPOT!

These strong horses have long been associated with farm work and once pulled ploughs across the fields.

35 POINTS

Thoroughbred horse

You can tell a thoroughbred horse by its sleek, athletic look. They are most often used for show jumping, horse racing and polo.

20 POINTS

Shetland pony

As the name suggests, these small horses originated in the Shetland Islands, north of mainland Scotland. Their miniature size makes them good for children to ride.

25 POINTS

American buff goose

The pale brown feathers and orange bills of these geese make them look similar to greylag geese, which you may be used to seeing by the river, though these are much larger.

25 POINTS

Embden goose

These white geese, with their distinctive orange bills, are the largest domesticated breed and notable for their upright posture.

20 POINTS

Muscovy duck

30 POINTS

With their distinctive red face and black-and-white plumage, this large duck is unmistakable.

Pekin duck

Large white ducks with bright yellow bills and orange feet, Pekin ducks originally came from China, where they were kept by boat people.

15 POINTS

Leghorn chicken

Known for being noisy and intelligent, these white birds are excellent egg layers – some hens can lay more than four eggs a week.

10 POINTS

Polish chicken

Don't be fooled by the name of this chicken as it originally came from the Netherlands. The crest of feathers on its head looks like an impressive hairstyle!

25 POINTS

Orpington chicken

Named after the town in Kent where they were first bred, these large, gingery-coloured chickens have a heart-shaped body.

10 POINTS

Cambridge bronze turkey

On first glance, these birds appear more black than bronze – but look closer and you'll notice their plumage has a definite brown sheen, especially on their tail feathers.

25 POINTS

Cockerel

You can tell a male chicken by the long, arched feathers of its tail and its loud cock-a-doodle-doo!

15 POINTS

Baby animals

Calf

Calves (baby cows) can be born at any time of the year, though you're most likely to see them in spring. Unlike a lot of other farm animals, it's very rare for a cow to give birth to more than one baby at a time.

15 POINTS

Kid

A group of baby goats (kids) is known as a tribe. They start walking just ten minutes after they are born.

25 POINTS

Lamb

Lambs are sheared for the first time around the age of seven months – their wool is much softer than the fleece of an adult sheep.

10 POINTS

Piglet

A female pig often gives birth to a litter of around seven piglets, though some breeds of pig can have as many as fifteen at a time!

20 POINTS

Foal

Foals (baby horses) are born with legs that are only a bit shorter than an adult horse's – this makes them a little gangly during the first months of their life, until the rest of their body catches up.

30 POINTS

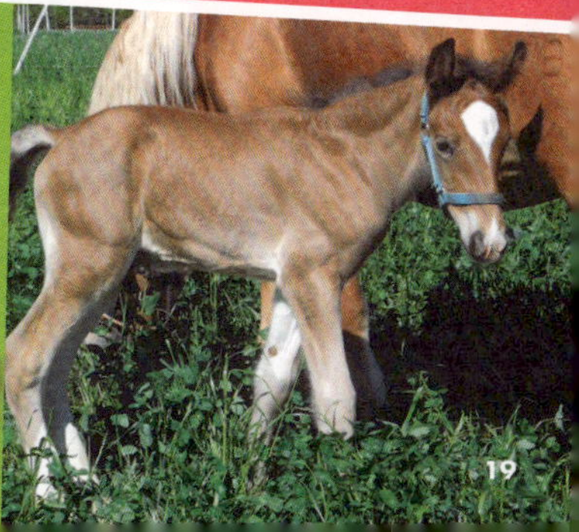

Baby animals

Duckling

Ducklings only get their feathers when they are around six weeks old. Before that, they are covered in a fuzzy down.

15 POINTS

Chick

Fluffy yellow chicks are one of the cutest sights on a farm in springtime. They hatch out of their egg using an egg tooth on their beak, which falls off as they get bigger.

15 POINTS

Small animals

Rabbit

You can often spot wild rabbits hopping around the fields, especially towards the end of the day, or you might be able to stroke them in a petting area. Lop-eared rabbits have long, droopy ears that are bigger than their heads.

15 POINTS

Rat

Rats have a bit of a bad reputation, but many people keep fancy rats as pets. They are very sociable and friendly animals.

25 POINTS

Guinea pig

Guinea pigs originally came from the grasslands of South America. They have no tails and are always happiest when kept in pairs.

20 POINTS

Chinchilla

With their soft fur, chinchillas make a great addition to a farm's petting area – though as they are nocturnal, it's very likely that they might be sleeping when you visit!

35 POINTS

Ferret

Ferrets were once used as working animals as they helped control wild rabbit populations, but today they are mainly kept as pets.

30 POINTS

Ice-cream stall

Some dairy farms make their own ice cream from their cows' milk – perfect on a hot summer's day!

20 POINTS

Play area

Farm play areas often include climbing frames, pedal tractors and big jumping pillows.

10 POINTS

Attractions

Gift shop

Stop at the gift shop on your way out of the farm and buy a souvenir to remember your fun day out.

15 POINTS

Café

Whether you need a snack or lunch, a café is a good place to rest and get more energy for the rest of your farm adventures.

10 POINTS

Arts and crafts

Activities like arts and crafts are often on offer, especially during school holidays, and allow you to make something pretty to take home with you.

30 POINTS

Pony ride

Riding a pony is a lot of fun as they are friendly animals. A grown-up will usually lead you and the pony around a small paddock or field.

25 POINTS

Animal race

Watching an animal race is always great fun – choose your favourite and cheer them on as they run along the track!

30 POINTS

Reptile house

Lots of fascinating creatures are kept in a reptile house, from snakes and tortoises to crocodiles. Sometimes they are so well camouflaged that you have to look closely to find them – under logs or along branches are usually good places to check.

35 POINTS

TOP SPOT!

Petting area

Here you can get up close to the animals by stroking or even feeding them. You can usually buy bags of special feed at the farm.

15 POINTS

Tractor ride

30 POINTS

A tractor ride will normally take you around the farm, and is great fun. If you sit near the front you can pretend you're the farmer!

Pick your own

In the summer it's often possible to pick your own fruit, such as strawberries and raspberries. Filling up a punnet is fun but you'll have to try hard not to eat them before you've paid!

30 POINTS

Machinery

Combine harvester

This big machine harvests, sorts and threshes (separates) grain crops. Look for them out in the fields in late summer and autumn.

20 POINTS

Tractor

Tractors are used for lots of farm work and can be big or small. They can pull, carry or lift things, and attachments can be added to make them even more helpful.

5 POINTS

Crop sprayer

These are normally attached to the back of a tractor and are used to spray crops with fertiliser (to make them grow bigger) or pesticides (to get rid of weeds and insects that might ruin them).

30 POINTS

Baler

A baler is used to compress hay into bales, which makes them easy to move and store.

30 POINTS

Plough

A plough turns the soil over so that crops can be planted.

20 POINTS

Planter

Attached to the back of a tractor, a planter sows (plants) seeds into the ground.

30 POINTS

Wheat

Wheat is mainly grown so that it can be milled and turned into flour, though it is also used as animal feed and can be used as an alternative to petrol called bioethanol. It starts off green but by autumn will be a golden colour.

20 POINTS

Oilseed rape

In spring, fields of oilseed rape turn a bright yellow colour. This crop can be used for animal feed or turned into vegetable oil.

25 POINTS

Barley

This cereal grain is used as food and in the brewing of beer.

25 POINTS

Oats

Oats grow particularly well in rainy countries and are used in lots of food, particularly breakfast cereals like porridge and muesli.

25 POINTS

Maize

This is another cereal crop, which by the summer months has such towering stalks that many farmers cut a 'maize maze' for families to explore (and get lost in).

30 POINTS

Sugar beet

The white root of this plant is used to make sugar – it looks a little like a bulbous parsnip, with big green leaves sprouting from its top.

35 POINTS

Field beans

These small beans are largely grown for animal food and grow rapidly in the summer months, with some plants reaching almost a metre high.

30 POINTS

Vegetables

Beetroot

This root vegetable is known for its vivid red colour. It is harvested in summer and early autumn.

20 POINTS

Brussels sprouts

These tiny cabbages grow on tall stalks and are a favourite Christmas vegetable. The top of the plant (called sprout tops) can also be eaten.

15 POINTS

Leek

Look out for rows of leeks growing in a field. They are part of the onion family but have a milder flavour. They're particularly good in soups.

15 POINTS

Vegetables

Rhubarb

Rhubarb's sweet flavour might make you think it's a fruit but its lack of seeds makes it a vegetable. You can usually see it being sold from April to July, and sometimes you can pick it yourself.

25 POINTS

Lettuce

There are many different varieties of lettuce, from green ones like little gem to the bitter red leaves of lollo rosso.

15 POINTS

Carrot

Carrots grow underground, with thin, frilly green leaves above ground. Though we are used to them being orange, they can also be white, yellow, purple and even red.

5 POINTS

Asparagus

This green vegetable is only available for a couple of months every year (May to June). Traditionally, British asparagus farmers stop cutting spears (the part of the plant that we eat) on Midsummer's Day.

35 POINTS

Vegetables

Broccoli

Though it looks very different, broccoli is actually part of the cabbage family. You can eat both the head and the stems.

25 POINTS

Cabbage

Cabbages can be green or red. Ones with crinkly leaves are called Savoy cabbages and have a mild flavour. Cabbages grow all year round but can get particularly big in the summer months.

15 POINTS

Fruit

Tomato

The tomato is classed as a fruit because its seeds are on the inside and it grows from a flower.

5 POINTS

Apple

We're used to seeing apples all year round in supermarkets, but apple season starts in autumn. Red apples tend to be sweeter than green ones.

10 POINTS

Cherry

This summer fruit grows on trees and often has a deep red colour.

30 POINTS

Pear

Pears are in season from early autumn to January. Most varieties have a yellow or green skin, but Red Williams are known for their red skins.

15 POINTS

Raspberry

If you're able to pick your own raspberries, you'll need to take care not to squish them as they can be very soft.

15 POINTS

Plum

You'll usually see plums for sale from late summer to early autumn. Purple plums are the most common but you might also find yellow and green ones.

25 POINTS

Strawberry

Strawberries grow low to the ground and ripen from May to August. If you're picking your own, look for fruit that are bright red all over.

15 POINTS

Cucumber

It's easy to mistake cucumbers for vegetables as we most often eat them in savoury dishes like salads. It takes them around two months to grow, and they do best in warm weather.

15 POINTS

Courgette

Part of the squash family, courgettes look very similar to cucumbers. They grow on vines on the ground.

20 POINTS

Redcurrant

These little red berries are very tart, so while you can eat them raw you might prefer them in a jam or jelly, where they taste a bit sweeter.

TOP SPOT!

35 POINTS

Blackberry

Another name for these juicy little fruits is bramble. If you're picking them yourself, watch out for thorns on the branches!

15 POINTS

Pumpkin

In autumn you'll see lots of different kinds of pumpkins, from the large orange ones that you might carve for a Halloween lantern to bright yellow and ghostly white ones that are good for cooking with.

25 POINTS

Gooseberry

These little berries look very similar to grapes (and come in both green and red varieties, too), though they have a more sour taste. They can be eaten raw or taste very nice in creamy desserts.

TOP SPOT!

35 POINTS

Bread

Freshly baked bread is often for sale in farm shops. A farmhouse loaf is white bread with a curved top, which is baked in a tin.

10 POINTS

Cheese

Lots of different types of cheeses can be made from animal milk, from hard yellow cheeses like cheddar which is made from cows' milk, to soft and tangy goats' milk ones.

20 POINTS

Jam

Jam is a delicious way to enjoy summer fruits all year round, and many farms sell jars of it made from fruit that has grown there.

15 POINTS

Milk

Fresh milk from the farm is much tastier than any you could buy from a supermarket, especially if you can find milk from Jersey cows, which many people consider to be the most delicious dairy milk.

10 POINTS

Chutney

Chutneys are normally served with cheese and can be made with fruits such as apples and tomatoes or with vegetables like red onion and beetroot.

20 POINTS

Pies

Freshly made pies are always delicious, especially when hot. As well as meat ones, farm shops often sell pies filled with tasty seasonal vegetables.

30 POINTS

Butter

A lot of farms sell butter made from the milk from their own cows. Butter is most commonly flavoured with sea salt but you might also find it with other flavours like garlic or truffle.

20 POINTS

Bacon

The two most common types of bacon are smoked and unsmoked. Smoked bacon often takes on the flavour of the wood it was smoked over.

15 POINTS

Yoghurt

As well as cows' milk yoghurt, you might find ones made from goats' milk and others that are flavoured by fruit from the farm.

25 POINTS

Produce

Eggs

Farm shops will often sell eggs from ducks and geese, as well as from chickens.

5 POINTS

Cider

This alcoholic drink is made from fermented apple juice. It might be sold in small glass bottles or large plastic jugs.

30 POINTS

Sausages

You'll most often see pork sausages for sale, sometimes flavoured with things like apple or chilli, but beef or chicken sausages might also be on offer.

15 POINTS

Wind turbine

Many fields across the country now have wind turbines in them, which create energy out of the power of the wind. It's a form of renewable energy that is better for the environment than traditional sources.

35 POINTS

In the field

Scarecrow

From a distance you might mistake a scarecrow for a person as they are often made of old clothes. They are supposed to frighten off birds who would otherwise eat the newly planted seeds.

25 POINTS

Hay bale

Usually circular or square, you might see them dotted around a field or piled up at the side, either bare or wrapped in plastic to keep them dry.

20 POINTS

Manure

If you spot a huge pile of manure (made up of animal poo), you'll want to hold your nose – it'll be very smelly!

10 POINTS

Sunflower

Fields of these tall yellow flowers are a stunning sight when they bloom in August. Some farms even offer the opportunity to pick your own sunflowers.

25 POINTS

Barn owl

TOP SPOT!

These birds can be hard to spot, but look out for them at dusk when they start coming out to hunt small mammals.

35 POINTS

In the field

Footpath

Many fields have footpaths cutting through them so that people can walk across them. This can be a great way to see fields up close if you're spending a day in the countryside.

20 POINTS

Pheasant

You'll often see these game birds in the fields. The males are a striking chestnut colour, with long tails and green heads, while the females are smaller and a much paler brown.

15 POINTS

Brown hare

A hare's long, upright ears make it easy to distinguish from a rabbit. They can also run really fast, which helps them escape from birds and other animals that might want to eat them.

30 POINTS

Drainage ditch

Look for these narrow channels along the edges of fields. They help to drain water from the land and are sometimes mistaken for little streams.

25 POINTS

In the field

Beehive

A beehive is usually home to between 20,000 and 80,000 bees, but there will only ever be one queen bee in it.

30 POINTS

Yellowhammer

If you see a flash of yellow in the field, it's likely to be this small bird, which feeds on seeds and worms.

30 POINTS

Poppy

These bright red flowers can often be spotted by the side of a field – or sometimes covering the entire field – in the summer months.

25 POINTS

Farmer

If you see a farmer they'll probably be very busy, as there is always a lot of work to do on a farm.

20 POINTS

Deer

You can often spot deer on open farmland, particularly towards the end of the day, though they'll usually flee as soon as they see humans.

30 POINTS

Lavender

Purple lavender flowers are especially popular with bees. They are prized for their fragrance, and their oil is often used in products that aid relaxation and sleep.

35 POINTS

Butterfly

Your best chance of seeing a butterfly is in the summer months. One of the most common types is the Peacock, which has eye-like markings to scare off predators.

15 POINTS

Windmill

There were once thousands of windmills in the UK but today there are only around 140, and most of them are no longer in operation. Windmills used wind power to grind grain into flour.

35 POINTS

TOP SPOT!

Greenhouse

These glass structures are used for growing plants in a controlled temperature, which means some things, like tomatoes, can be grown all year round.

25 POINTS

Chicken house

Also known as a coop, a chicken house usually combines indoor shelter and outdoor space for the birds. Its size will depend on how many chickens there are.

20 POINTS

Barn

Barns are one of the most important buildings on a farm, and can be used for storing crops, machinery and animals.

5 POINTS

Farm shop

A farm shop is a great way to try some of the products that are made on that farm, from fresh meat like sausages to homemade jams and creamy milk.

30 POINTS

Stable

This is where horses are kept, with each animal usually having its own stall. Larger stalls are used for mares (female horses) and their foals.

20 POINTS

TOP SPOT!

Grain silo

Usually large and round with conical roofs, grain silos are used for storing grain and seeds.

35 POINTS

Cattle shed

These open-sided structures are often very large, and are primarily used by cows during the colder months.

20 POINTS

Pigsty

These small, semi-circular structures are often made of corrugated metal. You might also have heard the word used to describe a dirty or messy room!

25 POINTS

Milking shed

This is where cows are milked. It is all done by machine now, but once would have been done by hand.

35 POINTS

TOP SPOT!

Buildings

Tractor shed

It's especially important to keep tractors in a shed in the colder months, to protect the machinery from bad weather.

15 POINTS

Farmhouse

The farmer and their family will often live on the farm in a farmhouse, which might be quite an old building. Smaller buildings on the farm might house other farm workers.

25 POINTS

Hand tools

Hoe

The blade of a hoe is set at a right angle to its long handle. It's used for stirring up the soil before and after crops are sown.

25 POINTS

Sickle

This traditional tool has a distinctive curved blade and is used for cutting grass (for hay) and cereal crops.

25 POINTS

Spade

You might recognise this tool from your own garden but it's also very useful for digging on a farm.

10 POINTS

Hand tools

Rake

A rake has many uses, including stirring up the soil, gathering together hay and crops into a pile, and clearing the ground.

20 POINTS

TOP SPOT!

Shearer

Sheep shearing is usually done with electric clippers, which look a bit like a very large electric razor.

35 POINTS

Wheelbarrow

Wheelbarrows are really helpful for moving things quickly from one part of the farm to another, and their shape is also good for mixing things like fertiliser in.

15 POINTS

Index

i-SPY How to get your i-SPY certificate and badge

Let us know when you've become a super-spotter with 1000 points and we'll send you a special certificate and badge!

Here's what to do:

- Ask an adult to check your score.
- Apply for your certificate at www.collins.co.uk/i-SPY (if you are under the age of 13 we'll need a parent or guardian to do this).
- We'll email your certificate and post you a brilliant badge!